A SHOAL OF POWAN

To Fiona

Happy Christmas 2018

from Andrew Geary

Andrew Geary

A Shoal of Powan

Rockingham Press

Published in 2018 by
Rockingham Press
11 Musley Lane,
Ware, Herts SG12 7EN
www.rockinghampress.co.uk

British Library Cataloguing-in-Publication Data

A catalogue record for this book
is available from the British Library

ISBN 978-1-904851-73-8

for all the Ware Poets

Acknowledgements

Thanks are due to the editors of the following magazines in which some of the poems in this collection were first published: *Acumen, Brittle Star, Candelabrum, Dreamcatcher, Envoi, Equinox, Magma, South, South Bank Poetry, Thames Poetry, The Interpreter's House, Ware Poets Darwin Poems Anthology, Weyfarers.*

'Dear Son' and 'The Boy with Three Fathers' were commended in the *Torbay Poetry Competition 2011* and *2014* respectively. 'Neptune's Staircase' was shortlisted in the *Bridport Prize Poetry Competition 2013*. 'The Order of the White Feather' won first prize in the *Broxbourne Council War and Peace Poetry Competition 2014*. 'A Thank You' won first prize in the *Wells Festival of Literature Poetry Competition 2015*. 'Ghostlike' won fourth prize in the *South Bank Poetry Competition 2016*.

I would like to thank David Perman of Rockingham Press for his kind and valued input throughout the publication process, and Frances Wilson for her excellent and evocative cover picture.

Contents

HOMING

Turning-out time at the loch-side pub
which sheds the only light for miles around
and we two, dull with beer, swollen with curry,
must pick our way like homing salmon back
along the rock-strewn shore to where we made
camp in the clarity of early evening.

And it is good, my friend, to pitch together
here in the Lomond oakwoods for a weekend:
me from the Thames but with my Shannon freckles;
you from the Clyde but with your Ganges skin,
your faithname Raju anglicised to Reg,
your large family, British for three generations.

Twenty fathoms down, a shoal of powan
moves like a blue whale in a million pieces
drawn by the moon, a memory of tide.
Shut in the loch these last ten thousand years,
the powan patrol, still itching for the ocean,
still (call them what you will) Atlantic herring.

CARLOS

drives a jalopy, *su burro*,
goading it through the gears
along streets paved with puddles,
his guitar stashed in the boot.

Hates England, *sombrío*
under its roof of cloud,
its plains of grey-washed houses
where debt and family fatten

while talk thins to *somero*.
The language doesn't sing.
He has Andalusian blood
and it needs to be shaken. So

when evenings lengthen towards *verano*
he drives his guitar into the city,
puts his fingers to work in a club
and renders such rhythm from wood and gut

that gentlemen and their dames *de dinero*
spring from their seats after desserts
to jerk like puppets to his strings,
to the music of the gypsy kings

and then begins the *fandango*
of the pound coins, from pocket to palm,
hopping like drops of golden rain
onto the velvet tongue of his

guitar-case.

SALIMA

I am *Salima, peace* in a woman's name.
I came to London as a refugee five years ago
when warlords took over my home in Mogadishu.
I work as a carer, looking after an elderly lady
who has become *Mama* to me. She also is a refugee.
She came here from Gibraltar in World War Two
when the sealords took over her home for their warships.

She has cable TV on which I am able to watch
the Somali channel. It takes me into Bakaara Market
where my sisters walk drenched in colour in flowing diracs
among stalls of cajeero, cinnamon, maraq, basmati, cambuulo...
I savour their memory, sprinkling their names on my tongue.
My brothers look on in trim white khamiis and western haircuts,
the younger ones playing meerkat to the camera.

Then I am taken into the city centre, past the hotel
where my parents used to stretch the afternoons
with long, lingering sips of Arabic coffee.
The colonial buildings retain their Italian good looks
even as ruins. In the streets of the Hamarwein,
my nephews play football using bomb damage for goalposts.
I hear lovesongs from doorways left open to look on the ocean.

Today I told *Mama* I must return to Mogadishu.
The old place is raising a smile to me through broken teeth,
its skyline flickering blue and white like the colours of our flag
through the window onto it here in a dark London living-room.
The English people are kind, but the concern they extend to me
is as embarrassing as a handshake, and sticky with questions
about Muslim extremism, piracy, khat, hijabs, infibulation ...

Why should I need to be concerned with these things?
I do not chew. I do not sail with pirates.
I am as my mother made me, and wear what she taught me to put on.
I read the Quran, and pray, and feel at peace.
There is peace of a kind returning to Mogadishu.
I want to add to it, as a trickle adds to a stream.
I want to return to *the Seat of the Shah*, to the sea.

THE MALECON

Lovers sit linked on the wall of the Malecon
lit by a vivid sunset. Intent on each other,
they would be nowhere else. A little beyond,
fisherboys seem to have the sea on a lead
as they cast, hold, retrieve, recast their handlines,
feeling the promise in the rising tide
as it draws fish toward the foot of the wall.
Perhaps there will be barracuda for supper.

Standing looking on, old men,
in the cracked but classical architecture of age,
remark how their energies have faded
like the pastel shades of the colonial frontage
of old Havana behind them. They were proud
when young to carry guns for the revolution.
Sentimental by evening, they tremble with memories.
The wall defines their home; they will die here.

But there are some, looking straight out to sea,
dying to be elsewhere. In front of them
the waves break, sending up walls of spray;
but it is not the sea holding them back;
they would take a boat tonight, its lights extinguished,
and head out across the Straits of Florida,
but for the coastguards with their ready weapons
and the sharks that take whoever hits the water.

A FAR CRY FROM BRIXTON

A lounge bar on a cruise ship's a far cry from Brixton,
an ocean removed from the taunts flung at a youth
called Freak, a dope epileptic, driven by the crack
of his own whip that lashes him somewhere inside.

Here, with his steel drums, in a pit of lights,
he hammers his angst into music, sets flying the tough-struck
notes like sparks, and sings with his driftwood voice
the redemptive, tripping songs of the Caribbean.

He has made Tourette's his unique instrument,
splicing the taser spasms of arm and neck,
the ejaculate *Yah!*, into his act – he is all
electric, delivering life-reviving shocks
to a genteel public, waist-length cable dreadlocks
jinking and jerking in their own rhythmic frenzy.

FAITH

Young Amani is grounded,
his feet cocooned in bandages,
yellowing flasks of infection.
Tiny fleas are burrowing under his toe-nails
like bugs under stones.
He is told that if he has faith, he will get well.

His room has one high window like a porthole.
All he can see of his friends playing football outside
is the dust devil they whisk from the baked earth
as they scamper around bare-footed, as he did
before the jiggers fouled him, brought him down.
He had dreamt of becoming Kenya's next Kadenge.

Now he dreams of becoming an airline pilot.
If he props himself up on his elbows, like so,
he can watch, through his window, planes on their flight-path
unzipping the stratosphere with their vapour trails —
comets, skytrains, jumbos, airbuses -
silver arrow-heads powering into the future.

This is the faith he has.
That one day he will shake off his sick-boots,
slip into uniform with shiny shoes,
stride out through that door,
be shown to an airliner decked in familiar colours,
seat himself at the controls, those starry gauges,

take off and climb higher than Kilimanjaro
leaving his room far below
small as a jigger flea
burrowing down into the skin of his past,
while he flies the national football team
off to World Cup glory.

THE DRINKING FOUNTAIN

The day is hot and difficult as always.

In the town square
    where the sun is boxed for people to enjoy
children wheel and catapult themselves
    while mothers and fathers idle on the benches.

Sequins of water glitter on the fountain.

A man pushing a girl in a wheelchair
    rickety-rockety over the cobbles
approaches the fountain, docking the wheels
    tight against the stone pedestal.

Lift me, Daddy! Lift me!

Her voice tugs and he bends,
    gathers her puppet body into his arms
and lifts – so light and yet
    so heavy, her fingers about his neck.

Press the button! she cries.

And for a spell of a minute or two
    he becomes her height and muscle and backbone,
his one hand on the button, his other manoeuvring,
    presenting her outstretched face, her goblet lips

    to the dancing water

that skitters over her skin, hops onto her hair,
    runs down her collar, doesn't know when to stop
and tickles her into rivulets of laughter
    that rise and swell, flowing out across the square

    till all the children stand still looking at her.

NEPTUNE'S STAIRCASE

Our small boat labours patiently
uphill, sixty-four feet in eight
assisted steps, progress that was
once thought impossible. It takes
an hour and a half to ascend

Telford's imaginative flight
from sea-level to the highlands.
One by one, the massive lock-gates
open their submarine jaws and
bloat the basin with a long, slow

intake of water. We wobble,
a bobbing toy in a big bath,
slippery high walls on either
side, while underfoot the floor churns,
rocks, and rises. But we win through:

with a gurgle of throttle and
snort of exhaust we exit to
the calm passage of the canal,
then on to the loch on whose still
waters we and our boat will sleep.

You are not with us here. Becalmed
by your recent stroke and growing
increasingly desperate (your
repeated phone calls exploding
into our skies like distress flares)

you have just manoeuvred yourself
on your one good leg, the other

dangling like a broken oar, to
the foot of a more prosaic
staircase. Upsurge of sheer Scots grit

will bear you up as you bump and
sway on a stiff climb out of your
own impossible. Gradually
a landing will come into view
with its tartan rug and pine door

opening into a thistle-
wallpapered bedroom. For the first
time in weeks, you will sleep in your
own bed, purple pillows and sheets
soft, scented, lucky as heather.

HOLY POOL

Why a skittering river that chuckles with trout
should suddenly fall dumb, deepen, and broaden
into this pool is a mystery.
                          Long ago
on nights when the moon was a quarter full and grinning,
the mentally ill were gathered here and driven
into the water. The pool became a Siloam
of the insane, a froth of hope and horror,
as the flailing ill were ducked and ducked again,
made to retrieve a bundle of stones for their cure
while their relatives, congregated along the banks,
scratched at the ears of God with their feeble prayers.

Back on land, the ill were coddled dry
then set in motion in a crazy clockwork,
circling round and round each of three cairns,
laying a stone each turn
                          till it was time
to be led a mile downstream to the priory,
to the flat slab under which the Saint was buried
on which was the Saint's Bed – a wooden contraption
to which they were lashed, the giant hypnotic eye
of the priory bell swinging inches above their heads,
a covering of hay on their racked bodies,
and there they were left for the night.
                                      Next morning
if the ropes had been loosed, the ill would recover.
If the knots were still tight ...
                          What most appals
is that there must have been, at the centre of all this
madness, one undeniable healing;
one unfortunate miracle must have occurred

to set false hope running amok among
a simple people.
                Somewhere along the strath
a lunatic restored to a right mind
must have settled down to keep a few sheep
while high up on the bens the unhealed roamed,
the great brass bell still ringing in their heads,
their wrists and ankles manacled with rope-burns,
their thoughts like bats flitting in hollow darkness.

RITE OF PASSAGE

Glasgow, mid-Seventies, strike-bound,
shorn of its shipyards, but still
with its king of slums The Gorbals,
a name that sounded like an infestation

to me and my brother and sister,
three Sassenachs in our touchy teens
being driven at night in the back of a van
for thrills through the streets of the city

by two Scottish cousins we hardly knew,
abandoned by parents to manhood,
Doc-Martin'd, white-vested, Saint-Christopher'd,
with accents you could sharpen a knife on.

All we could see through the van's rear windows
as we hung on while gravity failed us
were the sodium street-lights streaming away
behind like sparks coming off the roof

while Johnny Cash's *A Boy Named Sue*
growled from a hoarse cassette recorder
and smoke from a cigarette that flared
like a brake-light as it was passed round

giddied the air. When one cousin came on
to my sister, my brother started to retch
but nothing came up, and then a stone
hit the side of the van and we thought we were being

shot at. But the experience can't have been
that bad. Here we are, forty years on,
laughing like children about it as it slithers
and skids its way into, of all things, poetry.

DEAR SON

I trust this finds you in a sober moment
somewhere dry, out of this weepy weather.
Santaclaws just bolted in through the cat-flap
like a ginger missile, holing us afresh
with a flashback to happy times together.
The dogfox from the scrub must be dropping by.
Perhaps you have something of the fox in you,
stealing in today while we were not here
to sniff out money and disembowel the home.
We have smoothed over the gouged earth in the rose-tub
where you dug to retrieve the emergency key.
After what you have done, we have changed the locks.
We don't begrudge you the laptop and plasma TV
but what you trade them for may eventually kill you.
What you took is replaceable, but know
the broken things you left behind are not –
our nerves, our trust, our family dignity.
Your mother and I were daft to leave cash in the house,
in the same drawer as our most personal things.
Our wills – did you read them? Did you see
you are still, with your kid brother, an equal
beneficiary? We must have patience.
So long as I have two arms, there'll be one for each
of my two boys, though one play prodigal.
Tomorrow we face more questions from the neighbours,
the cutlery of their polite inquisitions
as they pick away at us. Let them ask you
directly; we have no answers. But then it wouldn't
be you; it would be the demon drugs talking.
May God and not the police arrest you, son.

Tenacious love,
your father.

THE MEMORIAL OLIVE

The night his boy died of the will of God
he slipped from the clutch of priest, family, farmhouse

and walked his grief up to the olive plantation
in the ashen moonlight.

Choosing a young tree on the breast of the hill
he set on it with a harvest stick,

beating the branches with such brute surprise
they spat their baby fruits like broken teeth.

Then he wielded himself as a weapon, wrestled the wood,
snapping it back to the elbow, back to the trunk,

sweat gleaming on him like an anointing,
hands bleeding, a pain in his thigh,

as he rocked, twisted, tore at, the tree
till in time he slumped, exhausted.

In the quiet that followed,
under a slow haemorrhaging of leaves,

he gouged a cross in the bark
and left it oozing.

Tonight, twenty years on,
he has gone out, as nineteen times before,

to the memorial olive.
The tree has grown again, but stunted, awry.

It stalls above him like a breaking wave
as he kneels and weeps for his boy.

THE BOY WITH THREE FATHERS

The first father has been substituted.
He has misbehaved in an adult way
that Mum calls *adultery*. Now he stands
on the touch line, watching from a small flat
he calls *my dug-out*. Nan says he was not
in Mum's league. The boy sees him at weekends,
which Mum calls *the away fixture*. She has
washed his name from her tongue as if he were
a swear word and refers to him as *your
father* in a voice which smacks of tooth-ache.

The second father is game on, game off…
Call me Dad, he tells the boy, on good days.
But on bad days, *No son of mine would do
that!* Nan explains *He is your stepfather.*
He is a bit like a step – square and cold,
with hair the colour of concrete. Nan says
Mum walks all over him, *but he is Mum's
support.* Sometimes he looks slant at the boy
as if he were afraid of him. *You have
your father's jeans.* The boy is vaguely glad.

Father number three is the one Nan tells
the boy about when she takes him to church,
which is like a school for old people. She
pulls the boy close to her, closes her eyes,
and with a trembly voice says *Hallo* to
our father Richard in heaven. Nan says
no-one has seen him yet, *but we can all
enjoy his presents.* The boy wonders if
the other two are aware of Richard
and what they'd say if he were to show up.

A KNOCKING IN THE PIPES

In tied accommodation in their adopted country
they watch on TV the agitations in their native land.
It is ten years and two children since they met there –
he from the agricultural west, she from the industrial east,
their coming together a token of the political union
being forged in a State as young and optimistic as they were.

Now the two halves of their native land
find they have differences too deep to mend.
There are riots in the capital, rigged elections,
tanks on the move, cross-border troops, downed planes,
and under the whole, like cracks, those incursive pipelines.
The two of them watch intently, but do not talk about it.

She is proud of what they produce in the east of her country –
steel and chemicals, cars and trucks and trains,
the largest aircraft ever built, satellites and rockets.
The husbands that file into the factories while it is still dark
and return home at night with chafed hands and beaten expressions
may be half-starved but they are men twice over.

He is proud of the grain basket in the west of his country
with which his people fill the bellies of the poor.
He looks at his wife and cannot help but think
that the heavy industry of her origins
is beginning to manifest itself in her physical appearance –
she is growing thickset, hard-veined, her skin a little oily.

In tied accommodation in their adopted country
they sit at east and west of the settee
watching TV from their separate viewpoints,
two children between them complaining of cold,
the inadequate central heating working overtime,
a nagging knocking in the pipes.

THE DEBT COLLECTOR

Woken at seven by
the suited cockerel
pecking loudly with the
beak of his fist at the
glass pane in her front door,
she gathers herself up
into the comforting
warmth of her dressing-gown
and checks on the children.
Good, they are still sleeping.

He knocks again. She peeks
through the blinds to see if
the racket has roused the
neighbours. Do they know of
the human subsidence
going on between her
walls? the stress, her gradual
sinking, the bills piled high,
heavy as headstones with
her name, her cold numbers?

He knocks again. And what
should she tell him this time?
that the divorce bled her
till all her finances
ran red? that two sparse meals
into three hungry mouths
won't go? that this amounts
to harassment? that his
charges alone would feed
her meter for a month?

He knocks for a fourth time.
Lord, forgive us our debts.
Debt is a nakedness,
a sharker's strip, rape by
instalments. Let him take
just enough of what he
wants from her to make him
go away – this time the
few pounds she'd put aside
for her daughter's birthday.

WASTE GROUND AT UPPER EDMONTON

Where traffic clots at the lights, turn right
and follow the mud on the road for a hundred yards.
Stop at the wire. Beyond
is tippers' territory. You'll see
that the fence put up to quarantine the place
has been turned into a drive-through.
But don't. They come by night,
to cock their tail-boards at the regulations.

The sore earth is pimpled with their rubbish.
Ruts run to shells of cars,
fridges, cookers, baths, toilets,
flushings of homes themselves piled one on another;
crates, sacks, all shapes of bottles and cans,
cylinders branded with the kiss of danger,
pipes, valves, the ruptured intestines of trade;
and everywhere white plastic like the pox.

The wind sneezes into old newspaper
and rears up to bully a line of gulls
in session on the high perch of a security lamp.
They are grey and white, the colours of old men.
Perhaps they are wise.
They have put all appearances on the tip,
pared life down to bare necessities.
Home's where you have all you need and this is it.

GHOSTLIKE

"My direction is simply, Enfield."
CHARLES LAMB, *letter to Coleridge, April 14th, 1832*

Come, when the traffic is quiet,
to Westwood Cottage, Enfield;
stand looking over what is left of the Green,
and you will see them – Charles
with his *poor dear dearest Mary*,
siblings shackled by family tragedy.

Her symptoms returned last evening –
a bent of despair in her talk that drew them
into a thick of gloom where Charles' attempts
to please and appease prickled like so many midges
and all he could do as the crockery crashed about him
was gather such things as she'd need in the asylum.

See them now, hand-in-hand, as they set out:
him with splayed little legs, slight as a farthing,
a stammering former clerk shaped by a stool,
his visible load the half of what he is bearing;
her with her defining accoutrement,
the strait-jacket, stuffed tight under her arm;

a stone's throw behind them, as always,
the slobbering neighbourhood dog of the itching ears
that follows because it remembers the taste of blood
that spilled on the floor when Mary stabbed her mother.
Charles is used to it, throws it a cursory glance.
C ...Come on, Mary. I'll look aft ... after you.

THE ROUNDABOUT

Dead centre of town,
the roundabout is wide and featureless,
just earth and grass,
round which we drive on our daily grind
at the wheels of our dizzy lives.

It is a no-man's island nobody crosses
except by car, the brakes some way behind,
usually late at night.
Tyre-tracks next day raise smiles, lines of a joke
everybody but the driver could see coming.

Somebody must set foot there occasionally,
be responsible for those embarrassing birthdays
hung out like dirty bedsheets for all to see,
reminding us the years are winding down
behind the repetitive clock-face.

But today, behold!
The roundabout is bright with resurrection!
Those worthy men and women of the council
have gone all Wordsworthian
and planted daffodils!

Winter is past, the sun has risen again
and summoned up a host of starry flowers
that dance on slender stems in the breeze we create
as we drive round and round the roundabout
in sheer exuberance this spring morning.

THE RED KITE

It was when Sandy skied his bunker shot at the 10th
distracted by Mitch pulling a sandwich from his pocket
that our eyes rolled upward and we first noticed
the rufous angel on God's blue fairway to heaven
blessing our back nine with its outstretched wings.

That's a red kite, said Rob, who knows his raptors,
and I'm sure it's not interested in us,
beyond wondering why we keep pitching
perfectly round white eggs into the air.
The kite is a bird of prey, not a bird of prayer.

(Though there are mystical elements to its behaviour.
The parish newsletter describes how it feeds on the humble
earthworm,
not as blackbirds do, all foot-stamping and red elastic,
but with marvellous grace, treading the breeze two hundred feet up
while it draws the worm out with the needle of its eye.)

Kites have been spotted picking trophies from the village dump,
put in Mitch, *they're not really killers, more scavengers.*
Like we're not really golfers, more retrievers,
responded Sandy, moving off to look for his ball
as the kite floated away over the woods behind the clubhouse

returning to a nest which, if we could see it, would surprise us:
a trough of twigs cushioned with wool and scraps of paper
and all things disthetic, wedged in an oak;
a bird of such display on the fairway
taking its rest and rearing its young in God's deep rough;

just as we return home, putting off our paraphernalia,

pulling on an old sweater with more holes than St Andrews
to relax in a broken armchair with the Saturday supplements,
in which we read with disbelief about a red kite
snatching packed lunches from the hands of local schoolchildren.

WHITE STORKS NESTING

I could wish, for the sake of a play
on words, that those large birds
nesting on the counterweight
of the tower-crane that stands
one-legged on the shore of the town
were cranes. But no, they are white

storks. What birth do they augur?
Another block of flats?
Something about them suggests
the district surveyor, and the crane
is a set-square hinting at
the height of what is coming.

The birds are unconcerned.
Their home measures up, at a safe
remove from danger, solar-
powered, with a penthouse view,
and only a short distance,
as the stork flies, to water.

And, though they do not know it,
they have positioned themselves
right at that spot on my journey
where I must look up to read
a road-sign. I see them. My load
of care becomes sheer feather.

GERALDO

As a boy in Gibraltar, he'd monkey up
a dizzy path from town to the top of the Rock
and watch the birds wheeling in the upcurrents,
see what the wind had snatched for its game of faces.
Seagulls were the eyebrows of old sailors;
eagles were young gentlemen's moustaches;
swallows the shy smiles of their ladyfriends.
Sometimes, an exhausted bird of passage
would fall nearby. He'd lift it up, take it
and sell it for a 'Queen's head' to a tourist.

Thirty years on, he is first to rise
in his London street each morning, stepping out
into a dawn of pigeons' dull alarms,
to walk to his work as a metal-spinner.
The pavement's littered but there are consolations.
Some mornings, the Queen with a shy smile
glances up at him from a crumpled bank-note
lying where it spilled and fluttered down –
money that didn't make it home last night.
He picks her up, tucks her into his pocket.

MURPHY

Your name offers you up to the caricaturists.
All your life you have lived in Camden Town,
a North London accretion of workaday Paddies
poorside of the refinement of Regents Park.

There is not a hotel on your street, but a hostel,
spilling drunks who might have been you or your father,
so you don't move them on when they doss on your doorstep
and skittle their bottles, fouling the air with curses,

and you don't condemn your brothers in the bookies
standing in the litter of what might have been
your week's wages, hands digging in pockets
to turn up a smoke to lighten the walk home.

What your community has is richness of humour,
laughter that has men shaking off misfortune
like mud from their boots, honest to who they are:
Irish tricolour - worker, sinner, penitent;

and they crowd the church for Catholic Mass to hear
the lilt of Latin spoken with a Dublin accent
and the rosaries like a wondrous spirit breeze
stirring the women bowed like a field of barley.

But that is as things were before Camden Market.
Just to think of it makes you call down fire
on punks, new wavers, goths, grungers, new agers,
their faces full of little metal insults,

bared flesh tattooed with the Devil's doodles,
all surface and no soul, like the celebrities

and nouveaux riches moving in because, with the Market,
Camden is happening! So house prices treble

while O'Connors, O'Neills, O'Shaughnessys move away
because they can't afford the rent and rates
and can't find a space to park their vehicles
and can't get near the bar in the themed pub.

A while back, the Market caught fire
and you stood radiant with righteousness
watching the purgatorial flames consume
the blighted heart of Camden. You hoped it would spread

like the Great Fire, putting an end to the plague
that had ridden in on the backs of the Market people,
but Murphy's Law proved true: it was soon extinguished,
the architects vowing to rebuild, bigger, brasher.

KEEP OFF THE GRASS

For all the urban sprawl,
browning of hinterland,
mown grass is still
the uniform of England,

a striped green blazer
for homes and schools and pubs,
a robe for public spaces,
a sports jacket for clubs.

Wherever you see mown grass,
slow down, savour its smell
which naturally surpasses
Dior or Chanel

and let your eyes recline
on it, or if you wish
run them along its lines
in a hundred metre dash.

But keep off it, please,
you who would see it sold
for housing. Take your thieves'
hands off our green gold.

KING HAROLD'S DUST

Youths on bikes saw through the Abbey gardens,
churning the dust of Harold, 'laid to rest' here
ten centuries ago, his grave's location
disturbed, divided by many subsequent moves,
his disintegration becoming as protracted
as that of Halley's Comet which chalked his death
on the night skies just weeks before the Battle.

The youths are so full of fight, had they been here
when Harold stabled at Waltham to pray before
its healing Cross on his way south to Hastings,
he'd have joined them to his army. Bikes are their horses;
prayer is a form of speech as foreign to them
as French to Saxon England; and Waltham Cross
is a place where some of them live, nothing more.

A breeze from the Lee Valley lifts the dust
the bikes have spewed across the Abbey paths.
The dust sticks in my throat, makes my eyes water.
I would be glad for a medicinal mist
to roll in from the river and hang thick,
with a damp grip restoring superstition,
aglow with a transcendence like the moonlight.

COMFREY

A weed but by no means weedy,
this plant is almost a lady among the lowlife
that nettles and prickles the towpath.

Tall, with a hint of curtsey,
she proffers her pendulous flowers
like a tiny hand with five purple fingernails.

Comfrey.
Here is her name in the book
alongside her windblown Latin companion –

Symphytum officinale.
He is quite a talker.
Half of it's Greek – *symphyo* – healing, uniting ...

The other half is a medieval story
of *officinas* deep in monasteries
where medicines were stored like bottled health.

Indeed there have been doctors in the family.
Unpacking her roots
yields *knitbone* and *boneset,*

hardened types
who packed out the sites of broken bones
rather like the plasters of Paris today.

Her own nursing credentials are impressive.
Leaves tucked like instruments into her stem,
she has one for drawing splinters, one for back-pain,

one to douse the flame of inflammation.
If pressed sweetly, she will link with liquorice
to deliver a serviceable cough mixture.

She will cut off her right arm
to boil you tea or Comfrey's cottage spinach,
reduce herself to mineral for your garden.

I am going to take her home with me,
plant her out, and with a sprinkle of good fortune
grow myself a servant-girl.

SPARROWS

are not well-loved. They boast
of no immortal roost
amongst the leaves of the
poetic canon. Their
diet is of scraps, as
is their nature. Feathers
of every shade of dirt,
they tip from hedges. Yet
there are lands to the north
where sheets of frigid earth
bear only needle leaves
and all that move are wolves.
The air howls for a whirr-
ing wing, the sparrow's chirp.

BURNING THE COLD

The field sweats mist
as it shoulders the cold.

Sheep pillow down.
A lone horse stands

head and back steaming,
branded into the landscape.

The trees are old survivors.
Their bare, blue-veined fists

defy the freezing sky.
They are already smouldering with spring.

Two lovers in the lane
rub heads together

telling in little bursts of smoke
how they burn for each other.

SUPERNOVA

How ordinarily the evening began,
cold and clear, November as it should be
in sixteenth century Denmark, Tycho Brahe
walking home from his laboratory,
the unchanging stars in their celestial spheres
reflected in the silver of his prosthetic
nose as he gazed skyward.

                                    Nothing shook
(but slipped a little further into sleep)
as one man's understanding of the world
jolted on its axis, Tycho observing
with naked eye –
                                    incalculably bright
in the constellation of Cassiopeia,
that beautiful vain queen of long ago
pinned by her five stars in the northern sky
upside down beside her husband Cepheus
                                    – a new star,
a prick in the perfection of the heavens.

When morning came, priests and philosophers
were troubled in their texts, the star appearing
to violate the daylight, brighter than Venus.
Tycho set to measuring with his quadrant
while the new star stood still over the birth
of a new age of doubt and uncertain motion.
Would the eternal prove ephemeral?
Certainties of the last two thousand years
paled away, even as the new star
faded and in eighteen months was gone.

Now that our eyes are everywhere and always,
space's superlatives fail to surprise.
How ordinary now is Tycho's nova,
shrunk to a neutron star just miles across,
brilliance reduced to blip, an invisible pulsar,
and though a test-tube of it would weigh as much
as a Himalayan mountain, frailest things
have become to us matters of greater substance.
Stars of today are human; gaze is inward.
Astronomers of the genes observe and chart
how dust holds together as living being,
a black hole at the centre of each one of us.

THE NIGHTWALKER

He has never belonged indoors. As he steps out
he feels small but free, a piece of superfluous
punctuation slipping away from its sentence.

The lit rooms of his neighbours at this late hour
are banks of TV screens, each household by evening
becoming a soap or sitcom. He wants no part in it.

Working into his stride, he comes alive
hearing his heartbeat played out on the pavement
while streetlamps make their own time with his shadow

first hurrying him on, then stretching him
as if he might, like elastic, snap back home,
before giving up on him as he goes through midnight.

He is putting the city and its stress behind,
strapped by its road-ropes to the valley floor,
its orange stain on the undersheet of the clouds,

and he is rising, floating, being absorbed
into the carbon blackness of the country
where the mud settles and the mind flows clear.

Complete in his own company, he walks
hand in hand with nobody at his side,
talking amongst his selves, wishing each *Good night!*

02:28

Freeze-frame stillness
over the floodlit expanse
of tarmac allotments
behind the 24-hour superstore.

Eyes watch from the wings,
the grainy edges,
galleries of leaves
on fringing poplar trees.

Suddenly a bird
mistaking the bright light for daybreak
bursts into song,
sets the whole scene whistling for its breakfast.

Bravo, hopping-happy bird
at incorrect o'clock in electric sunshine!
Ours is a world of many false dawns.
Bring on the singers!

A FENLAND HARVEST

Driving at night by fields fetched from the sea-bed,
dried in the stiff east winds and sown with wheat
that gleams in moonlight like a seam of coal,
I am surprised to see, so late,
flotillas of lights, to left and right,
great clouds of dust like dancing swarms of locusts
around the lamps of combine harvesters
working the fine weather.

To return by the same road next day
and see the hay bales strewn about the fields
like giant wooden cotton reels
and a played-out chequered board of stubble stretching
far as the eye can see
is to believe harvest is magical,
a game with Mother Earth she lets us win,
yesterday's rural idyll.

But all those lights and wheels so late at night
call to mind the industry of a pit-head,
surface sign of something seriously big,
and there are shifts of workers in the city
taking lifts to many different levels,
going to hidden faces, narrow employments,
lives kept busy bringing up the millions
that lie invested in these fenland fields.

THE SLAUGHTERMAN

advances through the herd of partygoers
embracing each one like a carcass. There is no
avoiding him. I squirm on the hook of his handshake
as he draws me in, bear-hugs me off the ground,

breath pressed from my chest as I engage
his bristly chin, blood-vessel cheeks, gristle nose,
bones of his gums that are his toothy grin,
his explosive *Gotcher!* as he sets me down.

Reaching the stage, he seizes the heavy accordion,
grapples it into his arms, begins to squeeze,
his fingers fasten on the white throat of the keyboard,
the instrument's belly sags, it coughs, convulses

and the hall is suddenly filled with delicious music,
a gambolling melody line, a pumping rhythm
and we are all dancing for the slaughterman,
jigging and reeling like there's no tomorrow.

WOLF!

I'm almost asleep to the radio
this holiday monday afternoon
when I hear *A wolf has broken free
in Broxbourne Woods* just a shout away!
The police are advising stay well clear.

I picture the woolly walky folk
who've gone down to the woods today
coming upon their big surprise
and crying *Wolf! Wolf!* while all
life within earshot ignores them.

I'll be falling asleep to the radio
again tonight when the air will be loud
with bleats of fear and phobia folk
calling the late phone-in from deep
in woods of their own where there's no-one to help.

Who can tell what's for real? But then
it's floating that question that makes the show -
a spinning coin that we don't see drop -
*heads it's a wind-up / tails there's a wolf
at the caller's throat* but we'll never know.

WRYNECK

They are back. We have seen one
crouched in its camouflage
low in the old sycamore
at the back of the orchard -

jynx torquilla, bird
that vanished from these parts
shortly before the dearth
that did for our forebears.

We have watched it, witch's puppet,
twisting and tilting its neck
as if to look up and back
at the hand that appoints it,

throwing its head back and shaking,
showing its pink throat,
guffawing in ghostly silence
over a private joke,

then suddenly *Quick! Quick! Quick!*
it speaks, like a squeaky wheel,
hurrying us to whatever
fate awaits us.

Since the bird's reappearance
we have looked at each other askance
with one eye over our shoulders,
troubled in all our plans.

FEEDING THE PIGEONS

The pleasure of feeding the pigeons in the square
   here beneath the city cliffs
      where the flocks break with a clatter of wings
        at your feet, my daughter!

The roaring traffic is trapped in its tides and cannot
   harm you here. You crumble the bread
      to a white shingle with shells of crust
        and cast it on the waters.

Your arms exclaiming, fingertipped with birds,
   rendered in bronze by the sun, you are made
      this moment's statue blessing the world
        at your feet, my daughter.

THE LEE-ENFIELD

My daughter holding a gun, remarking *it's heavy!*
One-and-a-half times the weight *she* was
when I first lifted *her* to *my* shoulder.
Her eye to the sight, taking aim.

The Lee-Enfield rifle. She'd rather her town
had given its name to a cheese, or a tart, or a pie.
The barrel is *rifled,* the old soldier explains,
to set the bullet spinning for greater penetration.

If she stands the gun upright, like so,
the point of the barrel reaches to her breast.
He takes it back, shows her the bolt, the breech,
how the square mouth is fed by the magazine.

It is, she concedes, a handsome object,
almost an antique, with its perfect finish,
ornate steelwork and walnut stock,
the colourful wood buffed to a baby's smoothness.

The old soldier warms to his charge,
tells her he has twice managed *the mad minute* –
thirty shattered targets in sixty seconds.
Seventeen million of these served twenty conflicts.

My daughter is quick with her maths.
Then if each one made was fired for one mad minute
with people for targets, that would wipe out
two-thirds of the population of Europe.

THE ORDER OF THE WHITE FEATHER

On active duty on the homebound platform,
  she spots a target, boards, sits opposite
  the young man not in army uniform,
waits for the carriage to settle, then slips the white
feather from her handbag and stabs at him
  like Kitchener's pointed finger. *Limp, or lame?*
Ain't you no fighter, cock? she barracks him.
  The young man reddens in a pool of shame.

Peace, when it comes, will not be as she planned.
  Shots fired in Sarajevo with local intent
sent accidental war through a continent
  like cracks through glass. Those fierce white feathers fanned
unready boys to Somme, Arras, Ypres.
The peace will be the quiet of men away.

ACKNOWLEDGE AND DESTROY

The replacements we are having to send you
are young and idealistic but have no idea
what lies ahead of them. We will remove
belts and ties from them before embarkation.
They are to join your advance division at night
when they will have only the beacon stars
to work out where they are.
                              Your seasoned troops
will shun them, considering they are filling
the boots of fallen comrades. They will be seen
as dead men walking. Some of them will fulfil
that expectation by being sent ahead
to navigate the minefields.
                              Six out of ten
will never fire their weapons in battle. Only
two in ten will be prepared to lead
any action of lethal consequence.
One in fifteen will desert.
                              They are not yet fit
so will tire quickly. The more tired they become
the more they will bunch while marching, and will offer
soft targets to snipers. Or they will present
with a self-inflicted wound, typically
a rifle-shot to the left foot or left hand.
You will notice a number of such tell-tale
casualties as fighting commences.
                              One day
the truth will be told, by those whose words will live
beyond their deaths. Look out for soldier poets –
wide-eyed types who will wander under fire
into the open fields looking for poppies.
Before you bury such, go through their pockets.

SILK HARVEST

Woken at dead of night by the drone of planes
she tip-toes to the window and peers out.
So many of them! - caught by the full moon's
searchlight in the gaps between the clouds -
waves of aircraft spilling paratroopers
into a running sky, an arriving front,
soldiers small as seeds hanging by gossamer
threads from the pods of their silk parachutes –
the Allies sewing themselves back into Europe.

Like a cat she watches them down. Some fall
among the cows who are dazed by the visitation.
Some fall into the flooded water-meadow
and thrash like shot swans against the sudden
weight they wear. Some fall into the poplars
and jerk like marionettes until they drop
or are cut free. Some fall at random angles
onto the barn. One falls into the hen-house.
She hears the rapid commentary of gunfire.

Gradually the noise rolls south, the air
clears and the sun rises over D-Day.
She slips from the farmhouse out to the fields.
Parachutes roil and ripple in the wind.
So many didn't make it! She skirts round
the tangled heaps, the mute protruding limbs,
nine men in a line drilled into the soil
still in their harnesses, and with quick snips
begins to gather in the silk harvest.

ARK ROYAL

Shaped like a great grey desk for the god of war,
its Harrier jets and Merlin helicopters
shrunk to Airfix models from the shore,
Ark Royal sails into the Bay of Gibraltar

past the redundant stump of Nelson's Quay
to which, after Trafalgar, *Victory*
brought his body in a cask of brandy,
when duty killed and drink came in for free.

Behind the ship's masts, high-rise flats display
Union Jacks like sheets on every balcony,
hung out to dry till Referendum Day
when the Territory as one will vote to stay

British. It's all slightly surreal:
this sea-power of a state that can't control
its fishing grounds; the admiral in his barrel;
this stub of rock beneath the Spanish *sol*.

But stand looking out from the siege-tunnel vents
in the veins of three centuries' resistance –
see how *Ark Royal*, even from a distance,
summons your pride, dismisses common sense.

HISTORY AND RAIN

She, oblivious to the lashing rain,
is bent over a bird-of-paradise plant
while delivering on the wind a potted history
of Queen Charlotte of Mecklenburg-Strelitz
from whom the plant derived its Latin name –
how Charlotte was uprooted from Germany
as a seventeen-year-old, driven through a storm
to a northern port, taken by British warship
through nine days of gales and sickness at sea
to a forced landing at Harwich, and on by horseback
to London and sudden marriage to George III;
how she had sought respite from the strain
of her fifteen children and her husband's madness
in botany, the tranquillity of Kew Gardens;
how this peace-flame plant was her favourite flower.

I, oblivious to all but the weather,
having been obliged to jettison the umbrella
that had threatened to parachute me into the bay
before snagging itself on the broken bones
of its own skeleton, am bawling at her
to get a move on before the gate comes down
as we approach the most exposed stretch
of the Territory, where Winston Churchill Way
makes its quick march across the airstrip –
which, if she wants some history from the boys,
was built for the Royal Navy with stone removed
whilst boring the war-room tunnels, the Rock unrolled
to a carpet on the ocean, now the parade ground
of the great Monarch bird, about to land
and lift us out to Luton, out of this rain.

History and rain. Perhaps that is how it happens.
Just a few drops of the millions that are shed –
tears of a queen, sweat of a frenzied king
or a toiling engineer, blood of a trooper –
coalesce; the mix begins to flow,
deepens across decades, finds one of its channels
here in Gibraltar, pooling round a plant,
coursing along a street it has given a name to,
levelling rock and carrying us before it,
confluence of history with the present,
the two of us together, clinging to each other
through rapids weather, another departure ahead,
somewhere behind us a bird-of-paradise flower
raising its pair of petals in a victory V
against the barrage of a winter rainstorm.

OLD MEN OF SPAIN

You would have thought
the housewives of Castile
had had a clear-out,
dumping all the old clutter
in lumpy, cloth-eared bundles
on their doorsteps.

The old men don't mind.
The weather's kind
and they are not old fools, but old fellows;
for there are many of them
out there on life's departure platform
and they're not going anywhere just yet.

In black berets,
they sit in companies
smoking the day down slowly like a pipe,
their conversation lingering,
swirling into laughter
long after what prompted it has gone.

When there is nothing to be said
they shuffle fingers step-by-step
into a game of draughts,
progress to chess,
or venture up a path of dominoes.
Win or lose, it doesn't matter.

They're easy going, although
you never see them go.
One day like any other
you find a doorstep freshly scrubbed,
its bundle gone,
a broken game-piece lying in the gutter.

LOOKING FOR MY FATHER

When he begins to fill my private space,
I go looking for my father.
Closer than you imagine, just out of view
beyond those gates that are locked each evening

is London's largest council estate,
a surprisingly green place, with neat terraces,
cut-flower gardens, candlelit squares
and flocks of angels roosting on the stones.

My father lies in an unmarked grave
somewhere in this suburb of the dead.
I think of him as one of the finally homeless
and wish he had an address, a front door,

if nothing else, his own distinguishing number.
There are a million here – how can I ever
hope to find him?
                    The place is quiet
but for the pleasantries of birds and breezes,

the hum of North Circular traffic
and revving of the cemetery bus
as it bears the living along
saintly-named streets between the tombs.

I have a favourite spot
down by Strawberry Vale Brook
where the water slips its culvert, rolls in the daylight
and itches itself on the sedge and willowherb.

I wait for the muntjac deer
that tiptoes across from Coldfall Wood
to drink in the late afternoon
every time I am here.

I think it is my father
stepping gingerly out of his hiding
to check on me, his glassy eyes
watching me while he sips, as was his wont.

BIG MAN

Big man, I champion your memory.
Ex heavyweight boxer, your life
was lived in bursts of compacted violence,
but I didn't know you till later,
in your retirement, your rented room
where you stunned me with that other
passion of yours – philately.

Gently over your boxes of stamps,
like an old silverback charmed by butterflies,
you'd sit through half the night
dipping your huge hands, that once
delivered a man to heaven with a punch,
your fingers sifting drifts of paper petals,
lifting them one by one into your palm.

That week of no reply in which you died,
they took you, boxed you, posted you
into a slot of earth in a London cemetery.
Big man, wherever you've arrived,
send just one letter home to us here
with a stamp from there. It'll be the first
of a new country in the catalogue.

There is so much we could learn.
Whose head will be on it – who rules there?
Will it show flowers and animals such as we love?
Do you celebrate days and anniversaries
or is time there not of any consequence?
The price will give some clue how far it has travelled.
A postmark, of course, would answer the burning question.

ARTS OR SCIENCE

"If I had to live my life again, I would have
made a rule to read some poetry and listen to
some music at least once every week."
                    CHARLES DARWIN, Autobiography

Darwin at sixty, addicted to science
and exhausted by the gravity of fame,
confided to a colleague that he would
love to hear Handel's Messiah once more
but was afraid his soul (whatever that be)
had shrunk too small to appreciate such fare.

In old age, he retreated into autobiography,
setting gently down on paper
burdens too personal for public airing:
loss of the higher tastes was loss of happiness;
laws and facts had trammelled lore and fancy;
why could he not endure to read a line of poetry?

Perhaps there is a type of natural selection
that turns each mind at school to arts or science,
one estranged from the other, though they be brothers:
Darwin the genius scientist unmoved
by deaf Beethoven's niagaras of melody
or dying Keats' everlasting verses.

LAST PUBLIC PERFORMANCE

His presence filled the hall with its resonance.
Here was Beethoven, huge as our expectations:
his *forte* frame, *crescendo* of greying hair,
grande proportions of his facial features,
and if you were lucky to be in the front row,
his *largo* hands, blunt but *prestissimo* fingers.

There were no visible signs of his deafness
except perhaps the exaggerated forward
bend of his body, as if that quiet burden
invisible to us was heaped on his back,
as if he peered over the edge of a private
precipice into the keys ...

                    But his playing! -
rendering ragged, common, his Archduke Trio,
the soft notes slipping away like dying children,
the loud notes visited on us like thumps and curses,
all on an out-of-tune piano. Here was
the disintegration of a virtuoso.

We had grown used to listening on earth
to a man who played from the heavens, a musical comet,
but this night we discovered ourselves in his tail
as the debris of noise, the dust of his genius,
flew into our faces, assaulted our senses
and stung our eyes as some shed tears for him.

What a mercy, then, he could not hear
how restrained and embarrassed was our applause
at the end of his pitiful performance!
Leaping up from his stool, he *Danke schoen!*'d
profusely, and bowed, his thick hair falling
over his forehead like a curtain closing.

VIRAL

i.m. Aylan Kurdi, d. ??/08/15

My lens, like a tabloid eye, zooms in,
cutting away the circumference
of cliffs, totemic lighthouse, swell,
for an intimate picture of the seals
at lounge on the cove's lunula
of sand. Bulls enjoying their cows.
Thirty or more. Consider, a mere
click or shiver from where I squat
three hundred feet away could trigger
a brutal stampede back to water.
Potentially fatal for the young.
A sympathy shot could go viral.

Another picture, another beach.
Something the size of a seal pup
before it grows the fur to swim
has been washed up. Zoom in. The bright
colours identify – red shirt,
blue shorts, grey trainers – a little boy,
one of the refugees. The sea,
as if ashamed of what it has done,
has nudged his body back onshore
and is licking his black hair. A policeman
lifts him gently without a word,
as if afraid he might wake him.

DISAPPEARED

They are dispatched daily from somewhere upriver –
corpses that swell with the current
and are carried for who knows how many miles
until they snag in the huddle of trees
that dip their skirts like widow washerwomen
on the long bend where our town draws water.

Fishermen pocket a few pesos to haul them out,
slide them like catfish into plastic sacks
and deliver them in beat-up vans to the morgue.

Most of the bodies are unrecognisable
except perhaps by articles of clothing
that still attach to them.

Birthmarks are gone, but there are deathmarks.
This one was a guerrilla – look,
shot in the side of the head with an army bullet;
this one an informant – he has no tongue;
this one a mule – wearing a signature cartel 'necklace'.

No matter, I check each one that arrives
to see if it is my lost property –
my dear one reappeared –
my late husband.

Most of the bodies are unclaimed
and are taken to the no-names corner of the cemetery
where their clothes are removed before burial
and placed in labelled crates by the cemetery wall.
One day a relative might recognise them.

You will think it strange
but I have taken a friend who helps to inhabit
the silence left by my husband.
He is a young man, of medium build,
with blue shirt, trousers with 32-inch waist
and size 8 brown leather boots.
Those clothes have lain long in his crate by the wall.

I have adopted him and named him Guillermo.
A simple plaque I purchased for his headstone
has the one word inscribed: CHOSEN.
I take wild flowers to him every Sunday
and sit back to watch the elastic swallows
coming and going through a gaping crack
in the slab that rooves his grave,
knowing perhaps much more of him than I do,
flying perhaps to where my husband lies.

A THANK YOU

You westerners burn your rubbish and your dead.
Our government burns our people in their beds.
Soon, if you want to see our tribe at all,
you'll have to go to the museum in the capital.

We knew it was our turn the night our dogs
were mysteriously poisoned. Only the demagogue
barked as his troops were ordered in to torch
our homes, our village school, our clinic, our church.

Forty of us escaped into the jungle –
I with my family, my little girl
losing us as she ran, my disabled son
working himself like a piston engine, his stump

paddling the air like a snapped oar, his brother
seizing his hand but only pulling him over,
my honey wife helping them up, mother frantic,
my aged father a bundle of sticks on my back.

We ate what was to hand, the forest's shakings:
grubs plump as berries; snakes we skinned
like lithe bananas; bark of trees; rodents
we stunned with stones; beetles, leeches, ants.

All but two of us made it to the border,
crossing the river by night on rafts that appeared
from the opposite shore. Like the dead freighted for heaven,
we lay still as sacks under a black tarpaulin.

The camp is comfortable but confinement is hard.
Your money feeds us rice and tinned pilchards
for which we thank you. Visit us! Come at evening
when the air is resonant with our tribal keening,

harsh circumstance drawing from us a song
like a blunt bow sawing a taut string
or the breath forced through a blade of grass,
such music from what little is left of us.

FLYING OVER AFGHANISTAN

Predator, an unmanned spy plane, transmitting pin-point pictures
of the movements of what appear to be bin Laden and his aides ...

cloud, over snow.
Forecasters cannot tell cloud from snow on satellite pictures ...

Captain Lucky, one of a crew of B-1B Lancer bomber pilots,
on a round trip of more than 5,000 miles ...

migrating common cranes, passing over the Salang Kotal
and up the Wakhan valley in considerable numbers ...

Psyops EC-130E planes, broadcasting US propaganda
on radio frequencies previously employed by civilian Radio Shariat ...

kites, flown by the kids of Taliban insurgents enjoying picnics and
                                                        barbeques
while they talk on cellphones to their comrades ...

a Chinook helicopter, at 150 mph and 25 feet off the ground,
a young soldier taking pictures out the back for uploading onto YouTube
...

a KC-135 Stratotanker refuelling aircraft, on any given night,
as soldiers in night-vision goggles move in on the enemy ...

a C-9 Nightingale air ambulance,
the wounded on stretchers in two rows stacked like bunk beds ...

red flags, flapping all around this mission, while children starve
                                                near the base camps.
They flag the possibility this deployment won't have the predicted
                                                satisfactory ending ...

Rob T, surname withheld, photographing from the air
the beautiful people and places while there's something left of them ...

a Boeing 747, on route from Bangkok to London,
the sun setting in the west ...

poppy harvest moon.
Shine on.

WAR VETERAN

No longer British Army but Salvation Army,
you are still six-feet-two-inches of straight-backed soldier,
but folded in a chair we help you into each Sunday.
Old age is waging cold war with your body.
Your sight is gone; a white stick insists on it;
but you wear those dark glasses and that rigid gaze
that have us wondering whether you are watching
some splendid private sunrise coming over your horizon.
The darkness is behind you. You don't talk about it any more.
We are most of us dead now, is all you offer.

Old man becalmed in blindness,
don't let what you have seen become history! -
the story that begins when the last witness falls silent
and truth is cut to fit the printed page.
Tell us once more of your work on the Siam Railway
when death came down the line before the train
and took half of your company on board;
how the Jap engineers, your tormentors,
erupted and spat like fat as they fried in their orders;
how you designed little explosions of your own to surprise them.

Reel off the work-camps like stations, as you used to –
the stink and splash and clunk of their infamous names –
Ban Pong, Sonkurai, Non Pladuk, Chungkai.
Recount the morning roll-call
when all the illnesses were found to be present –
beriberi, cholera, diphtheria, malaria, dysentery –
but five of the men missing, carried off by those illnesses;
how the evening was spent scratching together
a bonfire of bamboo to burn the bodies
because you had neither tools nor strength to dig graves.

Tell us of the monsoon rains
when the rise of water turned all resistance to sludge
and the river billowed into phenomenal life
like a vast groundsheet with a squillion rats running beneath it.
Tell us again why you ate whatever rodents you caught;
how the jungle shored you up with molasses and insects;
how the maggots were indistinguishable from rice
and made the rice heave, which made your stomach heave.
Tell us your joke about the camp music stopping
every time a Red Cross parcel came into the hands of your captors.

When you were liberated at the end of the war,
you weighed just seven stones –
a tarpaulin of skin stretched over a bone scaffold –
but enough, you said, for the Master Rebuilder to work with.
And here you are, tapping your shoes to the hymns
as you advance on heaven. Today, you hand me
a newspaper cutting – the obituary of an army colleague
who campaigned sixty years for compensation
for Far East POWs. *Nobody listened.*
It wouldn't have cost them much. We are most of us dead now.

GIBRALTAR PYRAMIDAL ORCHID

"Very rare … may have become recently extinct"
[Wild Flowers of Gibraltar, pub. Gibraltar Philatelic Bureau]

lately of Mediterranean Steps,
believed gone away,
keeping us guessing with her 'may'
like the prehistoric seas whose tides went out
but have not yet returned,
leaving the stony beaches of the Steps
high and dry
half way up the Rock and wondering why.

It was not expected of her;
she knew how to abound,
fond of limestone pavements and sea views;
from a large family of good name;
personally acquainted with Charles Darwin
who remarked how finely she was put together,
which, if science be given to sentiment,
tells why those butterflies and moths so loved her.

She may return. Look out for her,
tall and elegant among the grasses,
distinctive in her headgear,
her 'pyramid' or spire of stacked pink flowers.
Perhaps you will catch her fragrance on the air:
a faint suggestion of a fox,
sweet, musky,
gone before you know it.

BAOBAB

Were seed of a slaughtered elephant to take root
and be watered by a century of rains,
it would grow monolithic like the baobab,
a receptacle of myths and memories.

Having hacked tusks from the cheeks of elephants,
poachers secrete them in the baobab's trunk
out of sight till camels like creeping pyramids
pass by night to spirit them north through the desert.

Were poachers to be rooted to their crimes,
dug in beneath the baobab, they'd hear
and feel the fleshy thump, thump, thump,
of the falling ivory saucers of its flowers

that open at sunset, holding the light briefly
till bats in a frenzy for their nectar dislodge them.
Fallen, their scent is sweet for no more than five minutes.
How soon the air grows rank with their decomposition.

VIEW OF A WARTHOG

A burnt log
in the glassy heat of the plain
focuses as I close in,
becomes a warthog.

A four-legged Cromwell,
he poses for his picture,
short tusks curling from his jaw
like a bitten-through smile.

Then he puts bad looks to use –
lowers his shovel-shaped head
and digs in the dry river-bed
for roots and tubers.

Something disturbs his quest
(a lion in the wadi?)
for suddenly his low-slung hammock of a body
with a *hrumph!* and a kick of dust

is running at speed as if radio-controlled
with his tail in the air an antenna
tearing a trail of smoke across the savannah
then drops down a hole.

In the local language, Swahili,
he shares my name (with a hint
of a grunt in front):
ngiri.

YELLOW RIVER

Qinghai

High in the Bayan Har
where milk of snow fattens the royal streams
the peacock river displays,
irrepressible at its beginnings,
drawing its whirlpool tail along the valleys.
(But nomads talk of thinness of flow,
thinness of grass, thinness of yaks and sheep,
thinness of sleep as they listen through the night
to the thunder of silver iodide guns
needling the clouds to bleed them of their rain.)

Gansu

Bound by the lotus gorge,
the river learns restraint.
Here are bad omens –
drowned villages underfoot,
sunken balconies and stairs,
bones that prickle like rice.
The river is thrust up against a wall,
power squeezed from its innards.
It tumbles free, sparking,
charges away down the valley.

Ningxia

Without the currency of rain,
the desert creeps like debt.
Drawn up along the river-banks,
fields of sunflower, wheat and wolfberry
suck on the long straws
of their irrigation channels.
The soil is cutting loose,
casting off its clothing of vegetation
and running naked in the wind.
The river idles, stares.

Shanxi

It is like an unfortunate marriage,
this meeting of loess and water,
the river loading itself with the baggage
that it will bear to the finish.
Every view of the river from here on
will be jaundiced by this union.
Once its complexion was clear;
now it becomes like an old silk stocking
in which the life of the water itself
will struggle and kick until it is finally stifled.

Henan

The boom cities hallucinate by night,
their vivid reflections trembling on the water.
They are high, high on whatever it is
they have smoked in their long chimneys.
Day breaks smudged and sallow,
homes, factories, fields collectively
taking a leak, flushing out yesterday.
The river withers like a junkie's arm
veined with lurid blues, reds, purples.
Close to shore, it steams from its exertions.

Shandong

The river is varicose, septic.
It sits up from the plain
between the parallel bars of the levees
as though it were being wheeled on a long trolley
as quietly as possible to the sea.
Sometimes the trolley tips.
Tucked behind the levees
are the villages of hideous reversal
where people gasp like fish out of water
while the water in them turns their guts to rock.

Bo Hai

The delta is the palm of the river's hand
begging for help. Which way to the sea?
The stimuli of fish, crustaceans, birds
have all died. Flat in its own sludge,
it reaches out yellow fingers
that clutch at the sea's edge
but are being dragged back
by the river's dead-weight.
It is stuck in its own throat.
The mud will bury it.